LET'S TALK ABOUT

# Fostering and Adoption

## Sarah Levete

## Stargazer Books

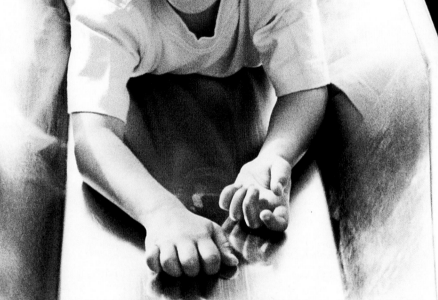

© Aladdin Books Ltd 2007

Designed and produced by
Aladdin Books Ltd

First published in the
United States in 2007 by
Stargazer Books
c/o The Creative Company
123 South Broad Street
P.O. Box 227
Mankato, Minnesota 56002

Design: PBD; Flick, Book
Design and Graphics


Picture research:
Pete Bennett & Rebecca Pash


Editor:
Rebecca Pash


The consultant, Shaila
Shah, is Director of
Publications for the British
Association of Adoption &
Fostering (BAAF).

*Library of Congress Cataloging- in-
Publication Data*

Levete, Sarah.
   Fostering and adoption /
by Sarah Levete.
     p.  cm. -- (Let's talk about)
   Includes index.
   ISBN 978-1-59604-085-4
    1. Adoption--Juvenile
literature. 2. Foster children--
Juvenile literature. I. Title. II. Let's
talk about (Stargazer Books (Firm))

HV875.L445 2006
362.73--dc22

2005057643

# Contents

# "What's my family like?"

There are many different types of family. Do you live with your birth parents, the mom and dad you were born to? Perhaps your family is just you and one of your birth parents. You might be part of a step family.

Sometimes, birth or step-parents are unable to care properly for their children. When this happens, the children may stay with another family, looked after by foster carers or adoptive parents.

Whichever family you belong to, the most important thing is to feel loved, safe, and happy.

In a foster family, foster carers look after and love a child until he or she can safely return home. If you are adopted, you live with adoptive parents who look after and love you for always, just as if you had been born to them.

You might be fostered or adopted or you may know someone who is. This book talks about fostering and adoption. It explains what happens and helps you understand how everyone involved may feel.

# "Why is someone fostered?"

There are many reasons why a child is fostered. It may be that their mom or dad has problems with alcohol or drugs, or suffers from emotional difficulties. The birth or step-parents may have hurt or mistreated their child.

A child is sometimes fostered if his or her mom or dad becomes very sick. Some children with very special physical or emotional needs may be fostered for a while.

If a mom or dad cannot fully care for his or her child, the child may need to be fostered for a while.

If birth parents are unable to look after their child properly, a person called a social worker arranges for the child to stay with foster carers. The social worker makes regular visits throughout the child's stay to make sure things are OK. He or she will discuss when and if the child can return home.

# Did you know...

Being fostered is sometimes called being "in care" or "looked after." Some foster children live with foster carers for a long time. Others stay for just a few weeks. Disabled children sometimes stay with a foster family to give their birth parents a short break. Whenever possible, foster children return to live with their birth parents.

# "What will my foster family be like?"

A foster family may be made up of just one foster carer or a couple. They may have children of their own who become your foster brothers and sisters. If possible, you will be fostered with your birth brothers or sisters. Your social worker can also arrange for you to see other members of your family. Over time, you may stay with several different foster families.

Foster carers are there to make you feel safe and secure when there are problems at home.

# Think about it

It's not easy being fostered—and it's not easy having parents who foster! If your parents foster, you may resent sharing your home and your parents' attention.

Chat to your parents about your feelings. Remember, there are loads of plus points! You'll make some great friends and it feels good to help others through difficult times.

Only people who can provide a safe and caring home are allowed to become foster carers. Social workers make sure that foster carers are able to offer the love and support you may need during your stay. You only meet your foster family when you go to live with them so there's a lot to get used to. It can take some time to settle in. But during your stay, your foster carers will treat you like the rest of the family, and help you feel at home.

# "How does it feel to be fostered?"

Many children who are fostered will have experienced great upset. You may have been hurt or have a parent who is unwell. Staying with a new family may feel strange and overwhelming at first. Try to be patient, it can take a while to get used to different rules, routines, and ways of doing things. Talk to your foster carers if you feel unsure.

It can take time to get used to living with a new foster family.

You may feel confused and sad about the problems that led to your fostering. You may feel angry and miss your mom or dad. These feelings are quite natural. Remember that foster carers only look after you until your birth parents can properly care for you again. Enjoying your time with foster carers doesn't stop you loving your mom and dad.

# My story

"My sister and I lived with a foster family for a while when Mom couldn't manage. Our foster mom and dad were great and treated us just like their own children. We could always tell our social worker about any problems and she still checks up on us. We're back with our mom now, who's finding it much easier to cope."
Thomas

# "Why is someone adopted?"

There are many reasons why a child is adopted. It can happen to children of any age, from all nationalities and cultures. If one or both birth parents dies, a child may be adopted. Step-parents might adopt their step-children so they have the same rights as birth parents. A baby may be adopted at birth if the parents are unable to care for him or her. If a child in foster care cannot return home, he or she is sometimes adopted.

Adoptive parents will look after and love their child as their own.

# Think about it

The birth parents of an adopted child have no rights over the child's life. Sometimes, children can have contact, perhaps by mail or phone, with their birth parents and other relatives. For others, it's best not to have any contact. Each situation is different and grown-ups such as social workers discuss what is best with each child.

Whatever the reason for adoption, adoptive parents care for and love their child as if they had been born to them. Adoption is not temporary— as long as the child is happy with the situation, they become part of the new family, forever.

# "Who can adopt?"

Some people adopt because they cannot have children of their own, or because they would like a larger family. Adopting a child is a huge step, and not just anyone can do it. People who adopt have to show social workers and adoption agencies that they can offer a child a safe and loving home. Children waiting to be adopted have often been treated badly, and may need lots of extra care and attention. Adoptive parents need to have plenty of love and kindness to share.

A relative can adopt a child, as long as he or she is the best person for the job.

# Think about it

Just like any other family, adoptive families come in all shapes and sizes. There may be one or two adoptive parents, or even two dads or two moms. A step-parent or a relative such as a grandma can adopt a child.

Whoever adopts, the most important thing is that they offer love, safety, and well-being.

"My parents are adopting a ten-year-old boy called Hashim. He's had a really tough time at home and stayed with several different foster families—but now he's coming to live with us! I'm really excited about having a brother and I'm going to make sure Hashim feels like part of the family."   Sunita

# "What happens?"

An adoption agency and a social worker make sure that the most suitable home is found for each child. They will consider the needs of both the adoptive parents and the child waiting to be adopted.

It can take a long time to find the right family to adopt a child. But when the right family and child are matched, a court hands over responsibility for the child to the adoptive parents.

A social worker makes sure a child is happy with his or her new family.

# My story

"At last I've got a new family! Yesterday I went to meet them for the first time. I was really nervous but excited too. They live quite near my school, so I won't have to change schools. I'm going to move in with them forever in a few weeks. I'm going to have a big sister as well as a new mom and dad!"
Elsa

While waiting for adoption, a child may stay with foster carers. Once the child is adopted, he or she may need to move to a new area, and possibly a new school.

# "How will I fit in with my new family?"

When you are adopted, you become a part of the new family. You probably take the family's last name. The family's uncles, aunts, and grandparents become your uncles, aunts, and grandparents. You may look different from your new family, but you belong to them, just as they belong to you.

Your adoptive family is chosen to make sure that you feel welcome and understood.

An adoptive family often shares a similar culture, religion, and language as their adopted child. This makes it easier for you to feel at home. When this is not possible, parents are chosen who will understand and appreciate your language, and cultural and religious background. All adoptive parents are encouraged to help you understand and respect your own cultural identity.

# 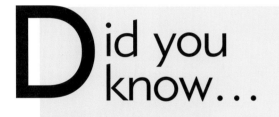 id you know…

Every year, almost 10,000 children are adopted from overseas into the U.S. These children have often suffered great poverty or lost their parents in war. Leaving their country in terrible circumstances can be extremely traumatic and their adoptive family needs to be especially supportive and loving.

# "How does it feel to be adopted?"

If you were adopted at a very young age, your adoptive family is all that you know and remember. At first you may not even know you are adopted—being told can be a big shock.

Many children feel hurt and rejected by their birth parents. These feelings are natural. Try to remember that your birth parents made the difficult decision to have you adopted, believing that others could offer you a better home.

You can have feelings for both your adoptive and birth families.

Even if you hardly remember your birth parents, it's OK to have feelings for them, whether it's anger, sorrow, or love. It's easier to deal with these feelings if you can express them. Try writing them down, or talk to your adoptive parents or close friends.

# Think about it

Your birth brothers and sisters may have been adopted into the same family as you. If they are with other families, your social worker can arrange for you to stay in touch. If birth brothers and sisters stayed with your parents when you were adopted you may feel resentful and rejected. Talk to your adoptive parents or other grown-ups about your feelings.

# "What about my birth family?"

If you have no memory or knowledge of your birth family, you may start to feel curious about them. Your adoptive parents will tell you what they know. Later in life you may decide to find out more about your birth family. Talk to your adoptive parents about this— they may feel anxious that you will no longer consider them to be your parents.

Your adoptive parents will tell you as much as they know about your birth parents.

# Think about it

People need to think carefully before trying to trace or contact their birth family. It's a huge decision. There are questions to consider such as: how will you feel if your birth parent doesn't want to see or talk to you? What if he or she is not what you expected? What do you hope for from finding your birth parents? Sometimes, teenagers or adults meet their birth parent/s and develop good relationships. But it is not always straightforward.

Finding out more about your birth parents cannot take away the care and love that your adoptive parents have given you.

# "Why is it difficult for me sometimes?"

There may be times when you will feel very aware of being fostered or adopted. For instance, birthdays might remind you of your birth parents. Sometimes, others may make unkind comments about being fostered or adopted. However hurtful, try to ignore such remarks—they are made by people who don't know what they are talking about!

Family arguments are just part of growing up and usually have nothing to do with being fostered or adopted.

It's easy to blame any problems at home on being fostered or adopted, but remember that all families have ups and downs.

Your foster carers or adoptive parents are getting used to you as well! Parenting may be new to them, so make an effort to get to know them and talk to them about how you feel.

# Think about it

Many adopted children look very different from their adoptive parents. This can feel hard, especially if others make comments about how similar the parents and birth children look. But feeling loved and happy is more important than having the same shaped nose!

# "How can I move on?"

You have two families, both of whom you can love. Your birth parents gave you life and your foster or adoptive parents show you love. You can have good memories of your birth family and your past. And you can have a new life with your adoptive family. Why not celebrate your adoption day, just as you celebrate your birthday? It can help you and your new family feel special and have a sense of belonging.

Try making a life story using words, pictures, and photos that chart your life from your birth to the present day. If you have no knowledge or photos of your birth family, simply write down or draw your thoughts and feelings.

If you are fostered or adopted, your start in life may not have been easy. But finding a loving foster or adoptive family is a time to love and be loved.

# Did you know...

What have the following people got in common?

A  Superman
B  Charlotte Church
C  Bill Clinton
D  Ice T
E  Eddie Murphy
F  Seal
G  Oprah Winfrey

A, B, & C were adopted; D, E, F & G were all fostered.

# "What can I do?"

- If you are fostered or adopted, remember that there are many types of family. Yours is no less a family than any other type.
- Talk to people about your feelings—they will understand what you are going through.
- If you know someone who is fostered or is waiting for adoption, think about how he or she may feel. They may be going through difficult times.
- If you know someone moving foster homes, or waiting for adoption, make a special effort to include him or her in games.

Be supportive of those who are going through difficult times.

# Contact information

If you want to talk to someone who doesn't know you, these organizations can help:

**Adoption Council of Canada**
Bronson Centre, 211 Bronson Ave., #210
Ottawa, ON K1R 6H5 Canada
Tel: (613) 235-0344
www.adoption.ca/

**Careleavers Reunited**
www.careleaversreunited.com

**Foster and Adoptive Family Services**
P.O. Box 518, 4301 Route 1 South
Monmouth Junction,
NJ 08852 USA
Tel: (609) 520-1500
www.fafsonline.org

**FosterClub**
753 First Avenue
Seaside, OR 97138 USA
Freephone: 1-877-216-7379
www.fosterclub.com

**Foster Youth Involved, Informed & Independent**
www.fyi3.com

**National Council For Adoption**
225 N. Washington Street
Alexandria, VA 22314-2561 USA
Tel: (703) 299-6633
www.adoptioncouncil.org

**National Foster Parent Association**
7512 Stanich Ave. #6
Gig Harbor,
WA 98335 USA
Tel: (253) 853-4000
www.nfpainc.org

**National Youth in Care Network**
332-207 Bank Street
Ottawa, Ontario
K2P 2N2 Canada
Freephone: 1-800-790-7074
www.youthincare.ca

**The Jim Casey Youth Opportunities Initiative**
222 South Central, Suite 305
St. Louis, MO 63105 USA
Tel: (314) 863-7000
www.jimcaseyyouth.org/

**There is lots of information about fostering and adoption on the internet.**

# Index

## Photocredits

The publishers would like to acknowledge that the photographs reproduced in this book have been posed by models or have been obtained from photographic agencies.

Abbreviations: l-left, r-right, b-bottom, t-top, c-center, m-middle

Front cover, 2, 3br, 4, 5, 8, 10, 11, 12, 13tl, 15tl, 17tl, 18, 22, 27br, 29 – Digital Vision. 1, 9, 15br, 21, 30 Getty Images. 3tr, 6, 7, 20, 25tl, 25br, 26, 27tl – PBD. 3mr, 17br – Corbis. 13br, 14, 16, 28 – Photodisc. 19 – © IOM 2002-MAF0101-Photo: Jeff Labovitz. 23 – Comstock. 24 – Linda Bartlett/NCI.